THE OZARKS

A Picture Book to Remember Them By

CRESCENT BOOKS
NEW YORK

1987 edition published by Crescent Books, distributed by Crown Publishers, Inc.
ISBN 0 517 62595 4
h g f e d c b a

They're beautiful hills, the Ozarks, completely surrounded by prairies, covered by rich forests, intersected by grassy valleys, undermined with natural caves and deep, cool springs, and punctuated by fast-running, crystal-clear streams. But the story of the growth of America had very little to do with beauty, and the masses of people who went west in the early 19th century by-passed this 200-square-mile section of northern Arkansas and southern Missouri because the very things that made it beautiful, the hills, the rivers and creeks, made it a natural obstacle. Besides, they are rocky hills and the soil is generally too thin for productuve farming. As a geologist of the time pointed out, "this is a region poor in material resources."

But what the Ozarks lack in material resources, they more than make up for in one of America's other really great resources: hard-working people whose customs and culture haven't changed much since their grandparents crossed over from Kentucky, Tennessee and Illinois after the Louisiana Purchase opened the territory in 1803.

The first people who roamed the hills were Osage Indians, who were conveniently moved down to Oklahoma to make room for the white settlers. They had coexisted with the French, who began arriving as early as 1700 and found a resource the later geologist possibly forgot about – lead. Though they've been digging it from the Ozark hills for more than two-and-a-half centuries, the region is still the largest producer of lead in the world.

By the time the Americans began arriving, the French had long gone, and the region was considered virgin territory. The best land was being offered for the incredible sum of $2.50 an acre and, except for a handful of rich Southern planters, nobody interested in going there could afford to pay such a price. The result was that the majority had to settle for the interior, which wasn't good for much, but was selling for less than 15 cents an acre. Many of the new arrivals had grown up in the Appalachians and had long-since learned to cope with hardscrabble farming. Though living wasn't easy, it was not impossible and they did know very well how to work. Their fathers had taught them, and they taught their children, and well into the 20th century, the way they worked, the way they enjoyed themselves, the way ran their lives didn't change a bit from the days when Daniel Boone showed them the way across the Cumberland Gap and settled along the Missouri River back in 1788. And though radio and television, automobiles and even airplanes have brought them up to date, the past still lives in the Ozarks in ways that don't exist anywhere else in the United States.

But the influence isn't entirely American. In the mid-19th century, waves of European immigrants came from Germany. There were so many of them, in fact, that there was a movement to make Missouri a German-speaking state. And in the mid-20th century, communities of Amish and Mennonites settled in the hills, multiplying the image of a population that doesn't set much store by modern technology and prefers a pair of mules to a hundred horsepower tractor any day, and never heard of, or couldn't care less about, the likes of Ralph Lauren and others preaching the gospel of comfortable elegance.

The idea of women's rights was slow coming to the Ozarks. From the earliest times, survival depended on a strict division of labor. The woman of the house has always been the absolute authority inside the house, and she and her daughters did everything necessary to make it run smoothly. It was her job to feed and clothe the family and raise the children. The man of the house did all the heavy work outside the house, and was in charge of the fields, the barn and the livestock, a responsibility he shared with his sons. The women often helped outdoors, of course, especially at harvest time, and the men did heavy cleaning work inside. But the worlds were separate, orderly, and the system worked without major complaint for the better part of two centuries.

Today we consider much of that kind of Ozark life to be "quaint," even "charming." But the people who live the life know it has been the only way to survive in this beautiful but hostile environment.

Today, the Ozarks is one the few places left where women get together for quilting bees, where the men gather at the general store to swap stories over a game of checkers and where the whole family gets together for an evening of community singing. It's where you can still hear the sound of a dulcimer, probably played by the person who made it, and where a square dance caller is better known than the man who reads the evening news on television. Though it's easy for most of them to get up to Saint Louis, where one of the world's great symphony orchestras has its home, they'd mostly rather stay home and listen to some sweet fiddle playing and the sounds of their beloved bluegrass music.

And for old-time religion, nothing on earth beats an Ozark revival meeting on a hazy, late summer day. Except maybe an Ozark wedding, which usually takes place at home, followed by a family dinner and a honeymoon trip over to the next county. The newlyweds can't stay away long. They have to be home for the shivaree, a noisy affair that involves banging pots and pans and firing guns to make sure the bride and groom don't waste a lot of time sleeping.

It is an America that was, the Ozarks. Fortunately for all of us, it remains as an opportunity to see what it was our grandparents had that made building the country possible. And in all of America there are few places as beautiful to watch how it all happened.

Facing page: Round Spring, Ozark National Scenic Riverways, Missouri.

The Lake of the Ozarks (top and facing page) is one of America's largest artificial lakes and was created in 1931 with the building of Bagnell Dam. Right: countryside north of Rolla, and (above) the Big Piney River flowing through the oak and pine woodlands near Rolla that form part of Missouri's Mark Twain National Forest, an area covering nearly 1.5 million acres.

These pages: the beautiful formations of the Meramec Caverns near Stanton, including (facing page) part of the Stage Curtain, which is the world's largest single cave formation and is thought to be over 70,000,000 years old. Overleaf: the Onondaga Caves near Leasburg, famed for their size and varied coloring.

Above: rock formations in Elephant Rock State Park, near Graniteville and (top and right) in Johnson's Shut-Ins State Park, near Lesterville, where the Black River flows through a chain of gorges called "shut-ins." Top right: Red Bluff, the great cliff at Davisville towering over Huzzah Creek, which meets Indian Creek at the old Dillard Grist Mill (facing page).

Previous pages: Rocky Falls Shut-In, in Shannon County, where Rocky Creek tumbles in a frothy cascade down a great, 50-foot-wide gorge or shut-in. The walls of the gorge are colored by purple porphyry and pink rhyolite, adding to the strange, enchanting beauty of the falls.

Above: the blue-green waters of Alley Spring, in Shannon County, flowing through the sluice gate of Alley Spring Mill (facing page). This handsome red building, dating from 1894, can work a saw-mill, generate electricity and produce 25 barrels of flour and 50 bushels of cornmeal a day.

Previous pages: Alley Spring, in Shannon County.
Above: a section of Norfolk Lake near Tecumseh, in
Ozark County, and (remaining pictures) the scenic
Current River, popular with canoeists because of the
speed with which it flows from its source in the Ozark
Mountains to join the Black River in Arkansas.

Previous pages: sun-dappled Round Spring which, despite its calm appearance, has a daily flow of 26,000,000 gallons of water. Right: Blue Spring, one of the larger springs near the North Fork of White River (top), and (facing page) Hodgson Mill, at picturesque Bryant Creek in Ozark County (this page).

23

Top and facing page bottom: Ray House at Wilson's Creek National Battlefield, which lies southwest of Springfield and was the site of the first major Civil War battle west of the Mississippi. Above: a ferry on Bull Shoals Lake near Protem, and (facing page top) farmland near Spokane.

These pages: Silver Dollar City near Branson, north of the Missouri/Arkansas border. The Ozarks of the 1880s are the theme of this exciting park, which features over 30 pioneer crafts as well as water rides (above and top) and the vast and beautiful Marvel Cave (facing page bottom right).

Table Rock State Park (overleaf), near Branson, came into being during the 1950s when a great dam was built across the White River, creating the 52,300-acre Table Rock Lake. Bordering the lake's northeastern shoreline, the park offers a wide range of water sports as well as some fine scenery.

Motels, clubs, diners and a dazzling kaleidoscope of neon signs line the main street of Branson (these pages and overleaf), a lively town at the heart of the southwestern Ozarks. Founded by Ruben Branson in 1882 with the opening of a post office store, the town became increasingly important as a trading post on the White River.

The coming of the railroad at the turn of the century, followed by the creation of Lake Taneycomo in 1913, accelerated Branson's commercial development and it now also serves as a major tourist center for its beautiful environs, which are characterized by high hills, deep valleys and tranquil, trout-filled lakes.

MUSIC ROAD MALL

Moe & Doe's
OZARK MOUNTAIN
GIFTS

Arkansas
Diamond Mine
JEWELRY & GIFTS

Bob A Lou Shop
TURQUOISE JEWELRY
REGISTERED DOLLS

Eggs-otic ARTS & CRAFTS

T-SHIRTS

OZARK & KENNETH'S LARGEST
OLDE TYME
PHOTOGRAPHY
350 COSTUMES 8 SCENES
PICTURE READY IN 90 SEC.
OPEN TIL MIDNIGHT

SIP'N'DIP
ICE CREAM
FUNNEL CAKES

Facing page bottom: a view of the lush, green landscape of Stone County, which boasts some fine Ozark scenery including tranquil Table Rock Lake (above). Top: the Highway 160 road bridge seen beyond the waters of Beaver Creek, which tumble over a small weir (facing page top) at Kisset Mills in Taney County.

Overleaf: fishing at Roaring River State Park, seven miles south of Cassville. This popular park covers 3,459 acres of Missouri and contains rugged, mountainous terrain that provides excellent recreational facilities. It also boasts an interesting past, for as late as the 1830s Indians camped and hunted near the Roaring River.

During the fishing season, the spring-fed Roaring River in Barry County's Roaring River State Park (above, right and facing page top) is daily stocked with trout (facing page bottom) from the hatchery of the Missouri Department of Conservation. Top: Long Creek, a southerly arm of Table Rock Lake, seen from the Highway 86 road bridge.

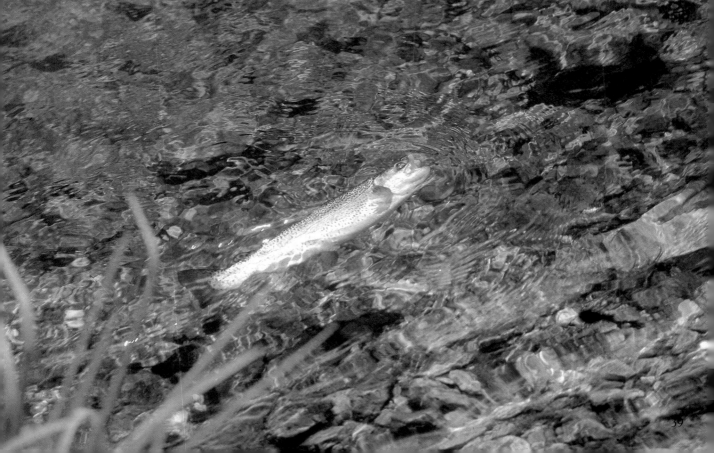

These pages: views of Table Rock Lake, showing (top)
Long Creek, a southeastern part of the lake, (above)
Kings River, which passes through the Viola area
(facing page) with its boat dock and forested parkland,
and flows into the lake's southwesterly stretches,
Overleaf: the evening sky over Table Rock Lake near
Kimberling City.

41

Left: an aerial view of the James River arm of Table Rock Lake, and (top) the White River winding away from the great Table Rock Dam (above) towards Lake Taneycomo (facing page). Overleaf: views of Table Rock Lake at Kimberling City, showing (main picture and left inset) Kimberling Bridge.

Left: jet boating, one of the many recreational facilities available at Mill Creek (top), south of Kimberling City, and (above and facing page) scenes of Dogwood Canyon, situated where Little Indian Creek meets Table Rock Lake in Stone County. Overleaf: sunset over Table Rock State Park.

Eureka Springs, Arkansas, sprang to prominence as a
fashionable resort during the late 1800s. Since then
the appearance of this charming Victorian town
seems to have changed little, and many of its
residential buildings, together with the entire
downtown district (these pages), are on the National
Register of Historic Places.

With its charming historic downtown area (top), Eureka Springs, Arkansas, is well-known for its wealth of tradition. Its main attraction, however, is the Great Passion Play, an annual outdoor drama performed in a vast amphitheater (above). Facing page: (bottom left) the "Christ of the Ozarks" statue in the Passion Play grounds, (top left and bottom right) the old Eureka Springs and North Arkansas Railway, (center left) the School of the Ozarks' chapel, (center right) Rocky Branch Park, Beaver Creek, and (top right) Beaver Lake near Bentonville, all in Arkansas.

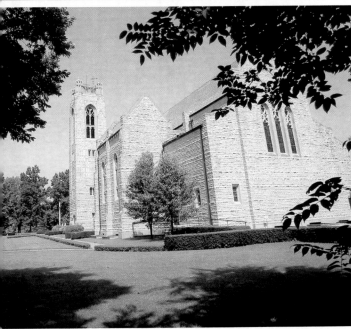

The Great Passion Play (these pages), which runs throughout the summer in Eureka Springs, Arkansas, is famous as America's top outdoor drama and has been seen by over three and a half million people. Opening in July 1968, it was first performed by 80 actors in a theater seating 1,200. Today, this lavish production is performed by a cast of 200 in a 4,400-seat amphitheater.

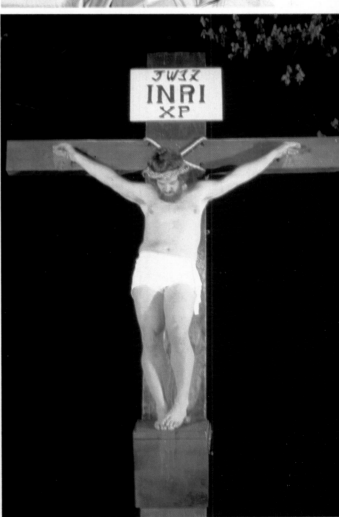

The play depicts the life, crucifixion, resurrection and ascension of Jesus Christ and, due to its realistic presentation, is powerful both visually and emotionally. Instigated by the late Gerald Ł.K. Smith, the Passion Play is now produced by the Elna M. Smith Foundation as one of several sacred projects including a re-creation of the Holy Land.

Above and top: farmland near Berryville (left). Facing page: (center left and bottom left) the main campus of the University of Arkansas, and (top pictures) the market, at Fayetteville. Bottom right: Lake Dardanelle State Park near Russellville, (center right) Prairie Grove Battlefield State Park, and (overleaf) Buffalo National River near Harrison, all in Arkansas.